AF504009

The rules and recipes in this book were collected by a homekeeper living in the 1840s. By this manuscript she ordered her happy home.

Women today, who may leave a few snapshots as the record of their lives, may wonder at the energy of someone who undertook a dinner party for ten alongside baking the household bread, curing its ills and collecting money-saving hints!

'The wise woman builds her house'.

*It is a useful plan to keep a tiny note book with pencil,
in the pocket so that every penny spent can be
put down and afterwards be entered in the
housekeeping book.*

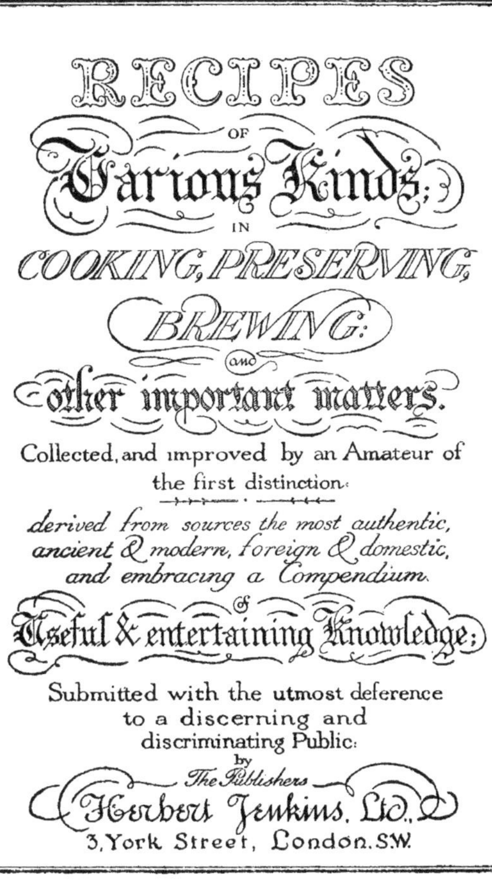
RECIPES
OF
Various Kinds;
IN
COOKING, PRESERVING,
BREWING:
and
other important matters.
Collected, and improved by an Amateur of
the first distinction.
derived from sources the most authentic,
ancient & modern, foreign & domestic,
and embracing a Compendium
of
Useful & entertaining Knowledge;
Submitted with the utmost deference
to a discerning and
discriminating Public:
by
The Publishers
Herbert Jenkins, Ltd.,
3, York Street, London. S.W.

ISBN 978-1-898617-46-4
A CIP catalogue record for this book is available from
The British Library.

*Recipes of Various Kinds forms part of a book published in
1927 by Herbert Jenkins Ltd. Herbert Jenkins Ltd is now owned
by the Random House Group. The 1927 edition tells us that the
title page and most of the recipes were sourced from a collection
'one hundred years earlier'. The material is reproduced here so that
readers today can enjoy these original recipes. Every effort has been
made to trace ownership of this collection. If any omission has
occurred it is inadvertent and should be brought to the attention of
Copper Beech Publishing Ltd.*

Copper Beech Gift Books
Copper Beech Publishing Ltd
PO Box 159 East Grinstead Sussex England RH19 4FS

WEIGHTS AND MEASURES
For cooks

Butter, soft (size of a small hen's egg).. 1 oz

Butter 2 tea cups ....1 lb

Flour 1 tablespoonful (heaped) ...1 oz

Sugar 1 teacup ....4 oz

English half pint ....10 fl oz

54 English gallons ....1 hogshead

BREAD AND PASTRY

Breakfast Bread

Put better than a quarter of a pint of yeast into 1 gallon water 12 hours before wanted, to take off all bitterness, then pour off water and mix it in a pint and a half hot water and half a pint of hot milk. Melt therein also by rubbing 1 ounce of butter. Beat up 2 eggs and mix these also. Then take a quarter of a peck of flour, more or less, so as to make the dough stiff in winter and slack in summer, mix this with the above as for pastry, but do not work it. Cover it up with a cloth to rise whilst you are heating the oven. *Let the oven be very quick, but not to burn.* Make the dough into Sally Lunns or rolls. Bake each a quarter of an hour on one side and then turn to bake a quarter of an hour on the other side. When done, scrape or rasp as you like best.

Delicious Plum Bread

Flour 1¼ lb, butter 2 oz, rubbed in, 1 egg, plums 8 ozs, (sultanas) 1½ teaspoonfuls baking powder which is to be put last. Bake directly.

Family Paste for Tarts

Flour 1¼ lb; rub in gently ½ lb butter. Mix with ½ pint water and knead or beat well.

Ice for Tarts or Pies

Beat up in a half pint mug, whites of 2 eggs to a solid froth. Lay some on the middle of the tart with a pastry brush. Sift over plenty of pounded sugar, and press it down with your hand. Wash out the brush and splash with water till all sugar is dissolved. Put the tart in the oven for ten minutes and serve up cold.

Note. All pastry that has to be iced, must be baked within ten minutes of its proper time, then taken out and iced as above detailed.

Wood Moulds for Pastry

1 lb flour to 2 oz butter. Melt the butter in as much boiling water as will be sufficient to work the flour into a stiff paste till it does not stick to your hand. Then knead it and use flour if sticky, till the dough does not rise on putting your finger to it.

Powder the board with flour tied up in a piece of muslin. Then roll out a piece of paste, not very thick, the size of the board. Press it well into the device on the board and with a thin pliant knife, pressing the left hand on the top, cut off the super-fluous paste, keeping the knife flat on the board yet none of the paste may remain on the board but what is necessary for making the device.

Should it not be perfect, press a bit of paste into the imperfect part and cut if off as before.

It is taken out by gently dabbing it in the firmest places with a small piece of the paste a little damped on the surface yet it may just stick, to raise the impression.

If the device is large it will require to be raised in several places.

Recipe for Exquisite Pastry

Lay 1 lb finest flour it on a marble slab. Divide 1 lb butter into four parts. Lay one part in the flour and sprinkle some flour over it. Roll it out with the paste pin so as to form a sheet of butter the thickness of a shilling.

Lay this aside and repeat with the three other pieces. Then take a piece of butter the size of an egg, and with your fingers rub it into the flour that remains *(best done in the basin)*. Add as much cold water as will make it a stiff paste. Roll this out the thickness of a penny, and spread over it half the sheets of butter. Fold up the sides and ends as you do a cloth. Roll it out again the same thickness, and put on it the remaining sheets of butter. Fold as before. Now roll it out again the thickness of a penny and cut the pieces of sheeting for the tarts or puffs with a tin cutter. With your finger press a hollow in the middle of each tart and put in the mincemeat)or other condiment). Bake for ten minutes in a brisk oven, taking care that they do not scorch.

Remove them from the pans when cool.

Useful and Entertaining Knowledge

A piece of bread or cobble of a peach may be put into the tart or puff instead of the sweetmeat and the preserve can be put in after. Iron ovens are more preferable to brick for pastry. Paste should be always made stiff.

In hot weather, put the butter in iced or cold water before using, and after the paste is made fold it in a clean cloth wrung out of cold water and let it remain half an hour.

A palette knife is the best thing for pastry and confectionery purposes.

CAKES AND BISCUITS

High House Biscuits

Boil half a pint of skim milk. Have ready some fine flour mixed with a little powdered sugar (1 oz sugar to 4 oz flour) pour the boiling milk hot upon the flour and work it till it is stiff enough to roll out as think as a wafer. Cut them out into shapes and bake them in a gentle oven and keep in a dry place.

Mrs. Jackson's Gingerbread Nuts

Flour one pound, coarse sugar one pound, treacle one pound, butter, free from salt, 12 ounces, ground ginger one ounce, a few cloves, a quarter of the peel of a lemon and two ounces sweetmeat.

Dissolve the butter with the treacle, sift the flour, spice, sugar and lemon peel through a sieve and bake in a slow oven.

Miss Marion's White Gingerbread

Mix ½ lb butter with 2 lbs flour, 1 lb lump sugar and 2 oz. ginger powder. Make it into a stiff paste with two eggs and as much cream as will make about half a pint. When well worked roll it out and cut it into small square shapes.

Mother's Lemon Cheese Cakes

Blanch a ¼ lb of sweet almonds. Beat them fine with a little orange flower or rose water. A quarter of a pound of fine sugar, sifted, must then be taken and having boiled the peel of a lemon in three or four waters and pounded it, add it and the sugar and the yolk of four eggs to the almonds. Then just before the cakes are to put in the oven add to the ingredients ¼ lb of oiled butter.

Line the pans with a thin crust and bake them for a quarter of an hour.

Crumpets

Make them of a thin batter of flour, milk and water and a small quantity of yeast only. They are poured in the iron hearth like pancakes into a frying pan, which they much resemble both in form and substance. They are very soon done on one side and must be carefully turned in time on the other.

Kate Henbury's Wine Biscuits

Mix ½ lb butter into 2 lbs of flour. Make it into dough with milk. Take pieces the size of a walnut and roll them out as thin as possible. Bake these in a quick oven a very light brown. Watch them carefully so that they do not burn. The more rapidly the whole is done the lighter the biscuits.

RECIPES FOR THE DAIRY

Wild Curds

To a pailful or so of cheese whey, boiling, put an equal quantity of buttermilk and boil together, when the curd will rise and must be skimmed off and put into a strainer.

Cream Cheese

To about six pints milk warm from the cow, put ¼ pint of cream and ½ teaspoonful of rennet. Let it stand 2 hours till it becomes curd. Then lay it on a sieve to drain until morning. Then put it on a strainer in the vat. Cover it with the strainer and lid and set a two-pound weight upon it. Let it remain till sufficiently drained. Take it out, put it in a cloth wet with whey and change it 2 or 3 times a day. *It must then be put in pewter plates with leaves till ripe.*

Yorkshire Cream Cheese

1 pint sweet cream from the top of the cream pot after it has been flooded (skimmed) 24 to 48 hours. *Lay a bit of calico in a basin.* Pour therein the cream. Tie the cloth up loose. Hang it up to drain 24 hours. Fold a dry cloth. Lay it on a shelf, place the wood frame upon it, lay a bit of fine strainer over the frame, scrape the cream into it, forcing it into angles. Cover the sides of the cloth over the cream. Move the frame frequently upon the dry cloth to absorb the moisture from the cheese. In 24 hours it will be solid enough to turn out and fit to eat. *Keep it in a cloth moistened with salt water and it will continue good for 2 or 3 weeks.*

Useful and Entertaining Knowledge

Fresh nettles or two pewter plates, will ripen cream cheese very well.

Cambridge Cream Cheese

New milk 6 pints. Only maw enough to turn it in 2 hours, putting it in when the milk is fresh brought from the cow. When come, put into the vat without breaking the curd, previously placing a straw at the bottom. In 24 hours put another straw at the top and over that a board. Turn the vat the bottom upwards so let it remain 24 hours more. Then flipping the cheese gently out of the vat, put it between 2 cabbage leaves and place it between 2 pewter plates. If the weather is chill, put it near a fire, turning the cheese every day. Use the same leaves throughout. In a week or ten days it will be fit to use.

Cheese Vat and Straw Cover for above
6 inches deep, 8 inches long, 5½ inches wide. Splines
at bottom at ¼ inch intervals instead of a holed
bottom. Board inch thick. Holes burnt in it.
Cut straws equal lengths and pass threads through
them across in 3 places and to unite them as to make
them serve the purpose of a cloth.

Sage Cheese

Bruise the tops of young red sage in a mortar, with some leaves of spinach, and squeeze the juice; mix it with the rennet in the milk, according as you like for colour and taste. When the curd is come, break it gently and put it in with the skimmer, till it is pressed two inches above one vat. Press it eight or ten hours. Salt it, and turn every day.

Stilton Cheese

Put the night's cream in the morning's new milk, with the rennet; when the curd is produced it must not be broken, as is done with other cheeses, but take it out with a soil dish altogether; place it in the sieve to drain gradually and as it drains, keep gently pressing it till it becomes firm and dry; then place it in a wooden hoop, and keep it dry on boards, turn-ing it frequently, with cloth binders round it, which are to be tightened as the occasion requires.

The dairymaid must not be disheartened if she does not quite succeed in her first attempt.

Useful and Entertaining Knowledge

In some dairies, the cheese, after being taken out of the wooden hoop, is bound tight round with a cloth, which is changed every day, until the cheese becomes firm enough to support itself. After the cloth is taken off, it is rubbed every day all over, for two or three months, with a brush.

Marigold Cheese

Pick the best-coloured and freshest leaves you can get, pound them in a mortar, and strain out of the juice. Put this into your milk at the time that you put in the rennet, and stir them together. The milk being set and the curd come, break it as gently and equally as you can possibly can, put it into the cheese vat, and press it with a gentle weight, there being such a number of holes in the bottom part of the vat as will let the whey out. The management afterwards must be the same as with other cheeses.

SOUPS

Bouillon, or stock

Take three pounds of beef, cut in shreds, put it into a copper stockpot containing four quarts. Fill it with cold water, place it before and *not on* the fire. Skim it while the froth rises, and when the bouillon is clear, make it boil gently.

Then burn on the charcoal a large red onion, skin and all. Being well toasted, throw it into the bouillon, with sufficiency of salt. After two hours add one carrot cut in four, two whites of leeks, one quarter of a parsnip, one head of celery, all tied in a bunch. Then add one turnip, one head of garlic, two cloves and a bunch of sweet herbs and some sorrel. *Boil this gently for eight hours.*

Any pieces of ham or bones that can be added will increase the excellence of the bouillon. The bouillon is passed through a tamis or sieve and set by for use. *In serving this for table, never boil.*

Useful and Entertaining Knowledge

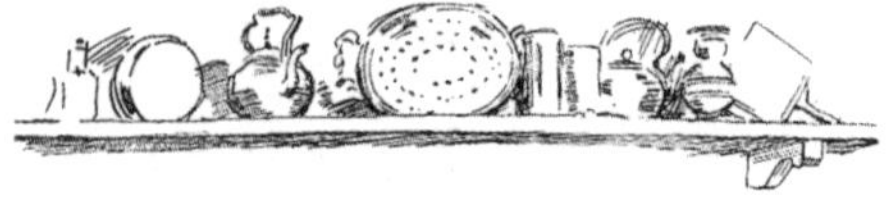

Thickening for soups

Melt an ounce of butter in a small saucepan.
When warm and melted, add flour to make it the
thickness of thick adhesive paste. Let it stand
heating by a charcoal stove some time. Then put
in the soup in the quantity of one spoonful to
two quarts. Note: this gives richness of flavour.

Glaze

All odds and ends of bones and meats, onions and
other vegetables. Boil all the goodness out and
strain through a cullender, then boil it down over
a quick fire to thick cream but so as not to burn.
Pass it through a sieve and colour with soy.

To clear gravy soup

Let the soup boil; then put in the whites of 5
eggs. After, force through a jelly bag.

Green Pea Soup

Boil the peas and pass the flour through a cullender as with other purees. Slice some onions and two handfuls sorrel leaves. Mince some chervil and pass the herbs etc. over the fire in four ounces of butter. Let the soup simmer a quarter of an hour and serve up. *Let some green peas float in the puree and add a lump of sugar.*

Scotch Hodge Podge (Improved)

8 pints water; boil it. Cut in small pieces 6 turnips, 6 carrots, 1 head cauliflower, 6 onions minced, 3 leeks, 1 head celery, ¼ pint preserved sorrel, ½ ox sugar and 8 teaspoonfuls salt. Simmer these 4 hours. Then put in a neck or ribs of mutton and in half an hour add a peck of green peas. In 2 hours it will be enough. Ten minutes before taking off, throw in a handful of minced parsley. The soup requires 6 hours' cooking together.

Carotte Puree

Take seven or eight tender carrots, cut them in thin slices, add some sorrel leaves, two sides celery and some chives or 2 cloves garlic. Put them all in a stewpan with a good piece of butter. Add enough water to cover them and a lump of sugar, half a hen's egg. Cover them up and boil them. When ye carrots are cooked and bruise easily, pass through the cullender and serve up as with other thick soups.

Macaroni Soup

Boil a pound of the best macaroni in a quart of good stock till quite tender; then take out half and put it into another stewpot. To the remainder add some more stock and boil it till you can pulp all the macaroni through a fine sieve. Then add together that, the two liquors, a pint or more of cream, boiling-hot, the macaroni that was first taken out, and half a pound of grated parmesan cheese. Make it hot, but do not let it boil. Serve it with the crust of a French roll cut into the size of a shilling.

Soup for the poor
The water in which meat has been boiled makes an
excellent soup for the poor, by adding to it vegetables,
oatmeal or peas.

Mrs. Soyer's Nine Penny Soup

¼ lb leg beef without bones, 6d   1½d

2oz dripping at 8d   1d

2 onions, leeks, celery and turnips   2½d

8 oz second flour at 9d   1d

8 oz pearl barley, or rice 6d per lb   3d

Total cost: 9d

Fry these together in a pan till of a light brown; then in a pot add salt 3 oz, and sugar ½ oz, water 2 gallons.

Simmer the whole together slowly 3 hours covered up, but stirring now and then. It will make excellent soup.

This soup is good for Poor and Rich.

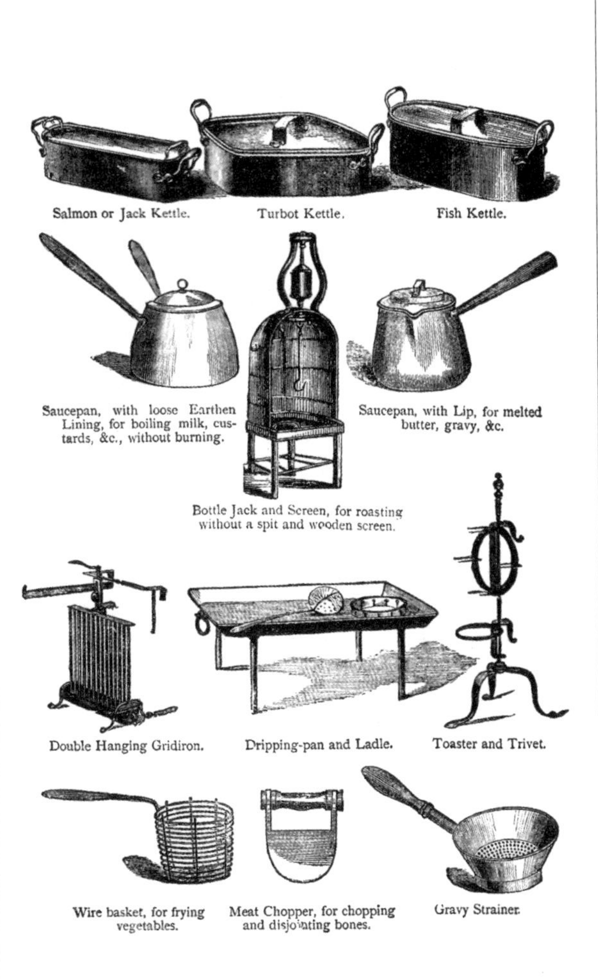

Salmon or Jack Kettle.

Turbot Kettle.

Fish Kettle.

Saucepan, with loose Earthen Lining, for boiling milk, custards, &c., without burning.

Saucepan, with Lip, for melted butter, gravy, &c.

Bottle Jack and Screen, for roasting without a spit and wooden screen.

Double Hanging Gridiron.

Dripping-pan and Ladle.

Toaster and Trivet.

Wire basket, for frying vegetables.

Meat Chopper, for chopping and disjointing bones.

Gravy Strainer.

FISH

Cod — the gill should be very red. The fish should be very thick at the neck, the flesh white and firm and the eyes fresh. *When flabby they are not good.*

Skate — If good, they are very white and thick. If too fresh they eat tough, but must not be kept above two days.

Smelts — If good, have a fine silvery hue, are very firm and have a refreshing smell like cucumbers newly-cut. They are caught in the Thames and some other large rivers.

Whiting —— The firmness of the body and fins is to be looked to, as in herrings. Their high season is during the first three months of the year.

Red Mullet

It is called the sea-woodcock. Clean, but leave the inside. Fold in oiled paper, and gently bake in a small dish. Make a sauce of the liquor that comes from the fish, with a piece of butter, a little flour, a little essence of anchovy and a glass of sherry. Boil and serve sauce in a boat and the fish in the paper cases.

To pickle fish

Split the fish down the middle and divide each half into six pieces. Make a brine sufficient to cover the fish, when in a saucepan. Season with pepper, mace and allspice, simmer the whole till the fish is done. Then take the pieces to cool and put them in a jar. Strain off the spice in which the fish was boiled and add to it a like quantity of vinegar and pour it over the fish, which must continue covered by it.

FRESH MEATS

Valuable Observations on Meat

MUTTON is the most delicate meat that is eaten. It also keeps best of any meat.

PORK is best between Michaelmas & March.

VENISON is best flavoured in August.

PIGEONS are best in September, in consequence of the great abundance of food everywhere.

POULTRY should be heated very gradually when put down to roast.

Useful and Entertaining Knowledge

All meat should be heated gradually.

A joint of meat may be preserved several days in summer by wrapping it in a linen cloth dipped in vinegar and sprinkled over with salt and then hung up, moistening it once a day.

Meats denote their being roasted enough when they throw out jets of steam from the joint.

Meats in roasting should have flour dusted over them just when they are nearly done enough.

Cooks are wrong to think that by boiling quickly they heighten the boiling temperature.

Beef-steaks and oyster sauce

Strain off the liquor from the oysters and throw them into cold water to take off the grit, while you simmer the liquor with a bit of mace and lemon peel; then put the oysters in, stew them a few minutes, add a little cream and some butter rubbed in a bit of flour; let them boil up once and have ready rump-steaks, well seasoned and broiled, ready for throwing the oyster sauce over, the moment you are to serve.

Leg of lamb with loin fried round it

Boil the leg in a cloth, very white. Cut the loin in steaks, beat them and fry them of a good brown; after which stew them a little in strong gravy. Put your leg on the dish and lay your steaks round it. Pour on your gravy and put spinach and crisped parsley on every steak. Garnish with lemon and serve with gooseberry sauce, or with stewed spinach and melted butter.

Mrs. Glasse's Cardinal Cook Rules

Roasting – 10 minutes to the lb for beef or mutton,
i.e. according to the fire and weather; as frost
requires roasting a longer time.
Pork – 15 minutes to the lb.
Pig – Fresh killed, 1 hour, otherwise add 15 minutes.
Turkey – large 1¼ hour, middling size, 1 hour,
small ¾ hour.
Goose – 45 minutes
Chickens – 45 minutes if large, but middling 30
minutes.
Ducks – 45 minutes if large, but middling 30 minutes.
Grouse – 25 minutes and bacon on breast till
frothed up.
Wild ducks – 25 minutes
Teal – 12 minutes
Woodcocks – 20 minutes
Partridge – 20 minutes
Pigeons – 20 minutes

Lamb, forequarter – 1½ hour

*To keep meat hot after being cooked if delayed serving, put it
in a Mary Bath covered with a cloth over all:
never before the fire.*

Squab Pie

Cut apples as for other pies and lay them in rows with mutton chops; shred onion and sprinkle it among them and also some sugar.

Podivies or beef patties

Shred underdone dressed beef with a little fat. Season with pepper, and a little shallot or onion. Make a plain paste. Roll it thin and cut in shape like an apple puff. Fill it with mince, pinch the edges, and fry them of a nice brown. The paste should be made with a small quantity of butter, egg and milk.

Sweet breads

Lay them in water, blood heat, three hours. Then blanch them two minutes in boiling water. Put into a stewpan at bottom a few slices of bacon fat, some sliced onion, carrot, parsley, a bayleaf, sweet herbs and a blade of mace. Add a little stock to half-cover them, taking care that sugar and salt has been put into the same and the usual proportions of a good teaspoonful of salt to each pint, and half as much sugar. Boil 20 minutes. Take them out. Dry them with a cloth. Egg them and add breadcrumbs and fry them a very light brown in lard in the wire pan. Serve with a white or brown sauce, or the liquor in which they were stewed, strained or thickened.

Sweetbreads are made to look handsome as a side dish by putting a piece of toasted and buttered bread under them so as to increase the apparent height and size.

Mutton Cutlets or Chops

Take best end of loin mutton. Cut it in pieces not too thick. Pepper and salt them before frying. Brown the butter in the pan, in which put cutlets till of a good colour. For sauce, take some stock; add to it 5 or 6 shallots, clove or two of garlic, spoonful or so of tomato sauce, a little vinegar and some herbs. Boil together a few minutes. Remove the shallots, garlic and sweet herbs. Thicken and pour over the cutlets on serving up, strewing thereon a few capers. *Clarified mutton fat: excellent for all savoury frying.*

34

POULTRY AND GAME

Boiled Fowls

Boil them in a good deal of water and skim well. It is better than putting them in cloths. A turkey takes 1½ hours if large, a small one 1 hour, a large chicken 20 minutes, a small, 15 minutes. Let the water be *boiling* on putting in.

Turkey with Truffles

Take a pound of truffles. Wash them in warm water till quite clean. At the last washing take a hard brush to cleanse them thoroughly. Peel them, put the peel apart. Cut them in pieces, afterwards mince the peels and mix them with a little parsley, chives, pepper, salt, the liver of the turkey, a little bacon and butter. Knead them together with the truffles and stuff the turkey therewith three days before it is to be roasted and set it up. Envelop it then in white paper oiled and roast in the usual way.

Chicken Salad

In the bottom of a salad bowl or soup plate, blanched lettuce hearts cut in quarters laid level. Arrange the white, the wings and the thighs of chicken or turkey thereon in form of a pyramid in the middle. Cut two hard eggs in quarters, place them round; near the top of the pyramid put five or six shredded anchovies. Crown the top with a piece of chervil, chive, cress and tarragon chopped coarsely. Make behind the eggs a string of gherkins and olives and round the dish garnish nasturtium. Season the salad before serving (but do not turn it) with 2 yolks of eggs boiled hard, four spoonfuls of oil, one and a half of vinegar and one of mustard, but little salt if there are anchovies, and a little pepper. These being well mixed together are poured over it at the moment of serving up. In winter may be added beet, celery, chicory according to fancy. The whole to be arranged with taste and symmetry. Some call this Italian Salad.

Tours, March, 1826. Excellent.

Goose Pie

Take a goose and a chicken. Bone them and see that the meat together weighs five and a half pounds. Then take two pounds of beef. Cut it in small pieces and with some sweet herbs dried and rubbed to powder, three leeks and three cloves of garlic seasoned with pepper and salt make up some force-meat. Lay some meat at the bottom of the pie. Then season it and put in a layer of forcemeat, and so on till the dish is full, the whole being seasoned with six spoonfuls of pepper and salt.

Giblet Pie

Put all giblets in a saucepan with 2 quarts water, 20 peppercorns, 3 blades mace, sweet herbs and a large onion. Cover close. Stew till tender, then put the beef steak at bottom of the pie dish, then giblets and liver. Strain in the liquor the giblets were stewed in, seasoned with salt and pepper. Put on the crust and bake 1½ hours. Add balls of flour and butter at bottom of the dish to thicken the gravy.

Pheasants

Give them plenty of water. Small ones will take half an hour; large ones, three quarters. Stew some heads of celery, cut fine, thickened with cream, and a small piece of butter rolled in flour. Serve with salt. Pour it over the bird and garnish with lemon.

Woodcocks, Snipes and Quails

Keep good several days. Roast them without drawing and serve on toast. Butter only should be eaten with them, as gravy takes off from the fine flavour. The thigh and back are esteemed the most.

Teal

This is a delicious bird when fat, which they generally are after a frost. They must be trussed with care like ducklings. They will take about eight minutes to roast. Serve with gravy, water-cresses and lemon, separate, about six on a dish.

Pigeons in jelly

Pick two very nice pigeons and make them look as well as possible by washing and cleaning the heads well. Leave the heads and the feet on, but the nails must be clipped close to the claws. Roast them of a very nice brown and when done, put a little sprig of myrtle into the bill of each.

Have ready a savoury jelly and with it half-fill a bowl of such a size as shall be proper to turn down on the dish you mean it to be served in. When the jelly and the birds are cold, see that no gravy hangs to the birds and then lay them upside down in the jelly. Before the rest of it begins to set, pour it over the birds, so as to be three inches above the feet. This should be done full twenty-four hours before serving.

This dish has a very handsome appearance in the middle range of a second course; or, when served with the jelly roughed large, it makes a side or corner thing.

SALT MEATS AND SUCHLIKE

To salt beef quickly

Beef 28 lb, salt 2 quarts. Lay the beef over a pan of water supported by 2 sticks to prevent the beef touching the water. Then place the salt on the top of the beef, covering it entirely. In 3 days' time, the salt will have passed through the beef and the meat is ready for cooking directly.

Hamburg Beef

Rub the beef well 2 or 3 days with common salt. Then make a brine with 2 gallons water, 1lb ham sugar, 1½ lb bay salt, 2 oz saltpetre. Boil and skim it and set it by cold. Put the beef into this 3 weeks, turning it every day. When the beef is to be boiled, soak it in water, warm, a couple of nights before. Use 3 ribs of beef.

Sausages

Take six pounds of a leg of pork that has been slain for 4 or 5 days. Cut it into thick slices; 3 parts lean to 1 part fat is best. Chop it as fine as possible: then add the seasoning: salt 1½ oz; pepper ½ oz; 2 nutmegs grated; allspice pounded ½ oz and a blade of mace. Mix well and put into a pot. Keep the skins in salt and water and change this water every 2 days.

Note. To each pound of meat put one teaspoonful of powdered basil leaves and this makes a fine herb sausage.

Oyster Sausages

Mutton one pound; beef suet one pound, oysters, one pint; yolks of eggs, four. Scald the oysters. Cut off the beards and hard part. Chop them small and season them with pepper, salt and mace. Then mix them up with the yolks of eggs, mutton and beef suet chopped fine and when got into the state of sausage meat put it into a pot and keep it for use, only rolling it up in the shape of sausages if skins are not used.

**Useful and Entertaining Knowledge
from a Lady of Kent**

Advice from a lady of Kent with whom Kate's cook lived and who was noted as the best possible curer and cooker of black meat in the country.

To cook a ham — Put it on the fire in cold water. Let it heat gradually to the boiling point. Then let it only simmer three hours.

To bake a ham — Cover it all over close with a flour and water paste. Put it in a vessel in the oven only moderately warm. Leave the oven door open for a time, so as to heat the ham gradually. Bake it till the crust beings to crack, which is a sure sign the ham is cooked, perhaps 2 ½ hours.

To boil a tongue — Put a large sized tongue in cold water, with plenty of pieces of any sort fat or good grease, on the fire, and simmer it gently seven hours. The fat mellows it.

A Recipe for making Bacon

This bacon is most magnificent when off a hog which weighed 25 stone. Cut the hog into 2 flitches. Pound 1lb saltpetre of sprinkle it on both sides of the flitches the night of cutting up. Leave it so till next day. Then rub it well in. Take about 12 lbs common salt. Rub in the same once a day for ten days, after which rub it every other day for 3 weeks. Then wrap it in paper and place it in a dry, but not warm situation. *If this should be troublesome in summer, put it into clean wheat straw and cut for use.*

Old Ham Economised

Take about 2 oz old ham free from skin and fat. Shred it fine. Beat a small blade of mace in a mortar and when in powder add the ham and beat all together with a tablespoonful of thick cream. Heat it well over a clear fire in the smallest size saucepan. Toast a slice of bread and butter when it is hot. Spread the beaten ham upon this thick. Put on it a few bread crumbs, on which put some small bits of butter. Salamander it and serve up directly. *Excellent.*

To Cook a Ham

If an old ham, bury it 3 or 4 days. If a new one of the year put in luke warm water over the fire and so remain till it simmers. Let it simmer very slowly, and when a skewer will pass through, it is done enough. Use plenty of water. 10 lbs ham takes 3 hours.

Mock Brawn

Boil a pair of neat's feet very tender; take the meat off and have ready the belly piece of pork salted with common salt and saltpetre for a week. Boil this almost enough; take out any bones and roll the feet and the pork together. Then roll it very tight with a strong cloth and coarse tape. Boil it till very tender, then hang it up in the cloth till cold; after which keep it in a sousing liquor, of wheatbran, sprig of bay, sprig of rosemary, salt and water.

FOR THE BUSY HOUSEWIFE

A Glass of Hot Milk

Taken in sips is the quickest restorative in fatigue and faintness.

Hot Water

Is a medicine within the reach of everyone. Half-a-teacupful as hot as can be drank comfortably half-an-hour before meals is a good preventative of indigestion; it is one of the best remedies for a disordered stomach if a little salt be added, and the same is the best gargle for a sore throat. Hot water is good for constipation if taken at bedtime; if followed up for a few months it will work wonders on the most delicate constitutions.

Bread and Honey

Taken for supper will induce sleep, and no better supper need be wished for.

To make Marmalade.

Boil Seville oranges till tender, and they can be pierced easily with the head of a pin. Cut them open, remove pips, separate pulp from rind, and take away the coarse parts of the orange and the white parts of the rind; cut the rind finely—pound some of it if you like—and add to the pulp. Now add about 1½ pounds of sugar to 1 pound of fruit, and boil till the mixture jellies. Some persons boil their minced rind and pulp, &c., in sugar syrup.

Apple & Suet Dumplings

Are lighter when boiled in a net than in a cloth; scum the pot well.

Lemon Sandwich Cake.

Take an egg, its weight in butter, flour, castor sugar, and ground rice. First beat the butter and sugar together, then add the beaten egg, and lastly the flour, with which a little baking powder should be added. Beat the mixture well, and divide equally, and spread on two buttered plates. Bake about 10 minutes, spread with lemon curd mixture, and press ligntly together. Sift white sugar over the tops.

Fish Toast.

Take cold boiled fish of any kind, pick into flakes, moisten with milk, add a good amount of butter, season with salt and pepper. When it is hot, spread on slices of buttered toast, and garnish with hard-boiled eggs cut in slices.

Rich Rice Cakes.

Beat the yolks of 4 fresh eggs for 10 minutes, put to them 3 ounces of castor sugar, work this well, then add 2 ounces of rice flour, 2 ounces of pastry flour, and half the grated rind of a lemon. Have ready the white of 2 eggs which have been whipped well, then beat altogether for some time. Place the mixture into a mould, and immediately into a brisk oven, and bake for about 30 minutes.

Little Short Cakes.

Rub into 1 pound of dried flour 4 ounces of butter, 4 ounces of white powdered sugar, 1 egg, and a dessertspoonful of milk, and make all into a paste. When mixed add currants, cut the paste into cakes, and bake.

Breakfast Cakes.

Take 1 pound of flour, ½ a teaspoonful of baking powder, ¼ a teaspoonful of salt, 1½ breakfast-cupfuls of milk, 1 ounce of sifted loaf sugar, 2 eggs. Beat the flour, powder and salt well together, and stir in the sifted sugar, add the milk and the eggs, which should be well whisked, and with the liquid work the flour into a light dough. Divide into small cakes, put them into the oven immediately, and bake for about 20 minutes.

A Good Light

The light of a lamp will be much clearer if a small lump of salt is placed in the bottom of the lamp in the oil. Also before inserting in the burner, soak the wick in vinegar, then thoroughly dry before using. This makes the wick last longer and give a better light.

Brass Work.

If brass has been neglected an ounce of oxalic acid added to a pint of water and applied to the brass with a piece of flannel will be found effective, and if well polished afterwards, the brightness will revive.

For Burns and Scalds

Nothing is more soothing than the white of an egg, which may be poured over the wound. This is more soothing than sweet oil. Cooking soda, with wet cloths laid over it, is also a good remedy for burns.

Borax

Placed in the water in which cuts or scratches are bathed softens the wounds, and cleanses them from all grit and impurity.

Lemons,

When they have had the juice squeezed out, may be dipped into salt and used to clean copper and brass utensils, a brilliant surface will be the result if polished at once with a soft cloth or leather.

VEGETABLES AND SALADS

French Salad

Chop three anchovies, a shallot, some parsley, put them into a bowl with two table-spoonfuls of vinegar, one of oil, a little mustard and salt. When well mixed, add by degrees some cold roast or boiled meat in very thin slices; put in a few at a time, not exceeding two or three inches long.

Shake them in the seasoning and then put more; cover the bowl close and let the salad be prepared three hours before it is to be eaten. Garnish with parsley and a few slices of the fat.

Fuller's Salad Cream

Take the yolk of three raw eggs; beat them up with sufficient salt and mustard. Then add five spoonfuls of oil and two of cream, with vinegar to taste.

Italian Salad

Two spoonfuls of mustard, two yolks of eggs raw, salt and a little pepper. Mix these smooth together, add little by little a spoonful vinegar, rubbing it round smooth. Then little by little in a small stream of 4 spoonfuls oil. A little sugar would round it on the palate.

At the end of each week, look over every item of expenditure to see if you have been extravagant.

Useful and Entertaining Knowledge

The fairins of potato is obtained by grating the root into clear spring water, where it sinks to the bottom. The liquor which is left is good for cleaning silk, cotton and woollen goods, as also painted wainscots. *Mrs. Morris, 1807.*

The farina is used for starch, but the lady above says it is an excellent substitute for tapioca in soup and milk. It is well known as the best thing of which to form souffles, and is sold under the name of *fecule de pomme de terre* at 4 shillings per lb. Potatoes boiled down to a pulp and passed through a sieve is very fine as gruel, and excellent for calves or pigs. An admirable size is prepared from potatoes, better than any other for distemper colouring, as it always preserves its whiteness.

Potatoes, how best to cook

Choose potatoes of equal size, put them in a pot without a lid, with water just sufficient to cover them, as potatoes give out water in cooking and being boiled without a lid they do not crack. When the water boils, pour it off and replace it by cold water well salted. The cold makes the heat go from the surface to the heart of potato and thus makes it mealy. A fork ascertains their being done enough. Then strain off the water and let them stand fifteen minutes to dry near the fire.

Mashed potatoes with No Lumps

Boil the potatoes or steam them, peel and mash them. To 2 lbs potatoes put 1 pint milk. Mix well; then add 4 ozs butter, well stirred in and serve up hot. Salt to taste. No lumps.

Potato Chips

Pare the potatoes thin. Cut in slices one inch thick. Then pare each slice round and round as thin as possible without breaking. Throw it into water as it is cut, till you have cut as much as is wanted. Then dry it in a cloth, after which it is ready for frying.

Green Peas a la Française

Put in the casserole some sweet good lard or butter; add some chopped parsley and a little sugar and salt. If the peas are naturally sweet, no sugar. Put them on the fire, and when cooked add a thickening of a yolk of egg or some rich gravy as most preferred. Serve up hot.

Ragout, Onions

Fry 4 good sized onions in 2 ozs butter till brown. Then dust flour over them to soak up the butter. Put them in a covered saucepan with weak stock enough to cover them. Stew them gently till tender (perhaps 4 hours). Then, having put them in a dish, glaze them. Stew the liquor in which they were cooked to a glaze also, and pour it over them for sauce.

Useful and Entertaining Knowledge

To Preserve Peas for Winter

Shell and put the peas into boiling water for three minutes. Put them in a sieve and when quite dry bottle them. Pour melted suet over the top of the peas. Cork them down tight and keep them in a dark cellar.

Kidney Beans for Winter

Put a layer of salt at the bottom of some vessel, then a layer of beans four inches deep. Sprinkle again with salt and then a layer of beans and so on till the jar is cramming full. Cover them over with a piece of bladder wetted and slatted, over this melted suet. Tie down close so as no air can penetrate and keep in a cellar till wanted.

To Dress Chardoons

Cut them into pieces of six inches long, and put on a string: boil till tender and have ready a piece of butter in a pan; flour, fry them brown and serve.

Or tie them in bundles:and serve as asparagus boiled, on toast, and pour butter over.

Or boil, and then heat them up in fircafree sauce.

Or boil in salt and water, dry, then dip them into butter and fry them. Serve with melted butter. Or stew them; boil as directed; toss them up with a brown or white gravy; add Cayenne, ketchup and salt. Thicken with a bit of butter and flour.

Stewed Mushrooms

Put them in a saucepan in as much water as will cover them. Simmer them an hour and a half till quite cooked and that the water has nearly steamed away. Then add cream, a dust of flour and pepper and salt to taste and serve up in a covered dish.

Sauté of Truffles

The spots where truffles grow, seldom grow anything else, as their root destroys almost all other vegetables and is mostly produced in grounds of a reddish loamy quality, buried about six inches in the ground. They must be sliced and dried soon after they are taken up. Having well washed and brushed the truffles, thinly peel off the outside. Then cut them in slices and, having melted enough butter in a sauté pan, put them therein seasoned with salt and whole pepper. Let the butter boil up 2 or 3 times and in about 2 minutes the truffles will be cooked. *Make a rich gravy sauce and serve them up.*

Pea Pudding

Boil the peas till quite tender, then take them out the cloth and stir them well together with a good piece of butter and salt and pepper to taste. Braid it quite smooth. Tie it up tight again. Boil it an hour longer and serve up.

Frying herbs as dressed in Staffordshire

Clean and drain a good quantity of spinach-leaves, two large handfuls of parsley and a handful of green onions. Chop the parsley and onions, and sprinkle them among the spinach. Set them all on to stew with some salt and a bit of butter the size of a walnut: shake the pan when it begins to grow warm and let it be closely covered over a slow stove till done enough. It is served with slices of broiled calves' liver, small rashers of bacon, and eggs fried, the latter on the herbs, the other in a separate dish.

PUDDINGS AND SWEETS

Rice Pudding

Boil one quart of cream, put therein half a pound of sugar, three quarters of a pound of rice. When the rice is swelled, melt therein a quarter of a pound of butter, add the peel of a lemon minced (and a little nutmeg). When the rice is cold, put to it four eggs, and four more whites. Then butter a mould wherein must be put at bottom some sliced crumb of bread, which is to prevent the rice from sticking. Put this into the oven half an hour before serving. *Do not turn it out of the mould till the pudding is going to table.*

John Hall Pudding

Macaroni 4 oz, boiled till tender in milk. Flavour it with bitter almonds. Cover a dish with ¾ of the paste and put at the bottom a layer of apricot marmalade. Pour over the whole a rich custard to fill the dish withal. Bake it 2 hours, turn it out. Spread the top with apricot jam and serve up.

Grandmother's Blancmange

Cream, one quart; isinglass, one ounce; sweet almonds (with seven apricot kernels) two ounces: well beaten; sugar to taste, a small piece of lemon peel. Put altogether on the fire. When it boils take it off and pass it through a sieve. Keep stirring till almost cold and then add a glass of mountain wine. Dip the mould in cold water and put in the blancmange.

Flummery which is Very Good

Put three large handfuls of very small white oatmeal to steep a day and night in cold water. Pour it off clear, and add as much more water and let it stand the same time. Strain it through a fine hair sieve, and boil it till it be as thick as hasty pudding; stirring it well all the time. When first strained, put in one large spoonful of white sugar, and two of orange-flower water. Pour it into shallow dishes; and serve to eat with cyder, milk or cream and sugar.

Norfolk Drop Dumplings

Make a thick batter with half a pint of milk, 2 eggs, a little salt, and flour. Beat it well. Have ready a saucepan with some milk and water boiling fast. Drop batter in with a spoon. Boil 3 minutes. Drain on a sieve and serve up on a napkin.

Batter Puddings

Take a quart of milk; beat up six eggs and three whites. Mix with them the milk and six spoonfuls of flour and a teaspoonful of salt. Beat it well together and boil it an hour and a quarter. Pour melted butter over it. Eight eggs and half a pound of currants will make a change if wanted.

Begnets

Put 6 good spoonfuls flour, 2 yolks of eggs, a pinch of salt, and of sugar, four spoonfuls of olive oil into a basin. Add by little and little a tumbler of soft water. Beat all together so that the flour and eggs should work quite smooth. Then take the whites of 6 eggs, beat them firm to snow and mix them with the rest: but take care to work them so as not to dissolve the solidity of the whites. Drop small spoonfuls of this batter into the frying wire pan, one after the other, as the lard is boiling in the frying pan. When of a yellow colour remove them, powder them with sugar and serve quite hot. Note. If the lard does not boil, the begnet will all be imbibed with grease.

Bockings

Mix three ounces of buck-wheat flour with a teacupful of warm milk, and a spoonful of yeast. Let it rise before the fire about an hour; then mix four eggs well beaten and as much milk as will make the batter the usual thickness for pancakes and fry them the same.

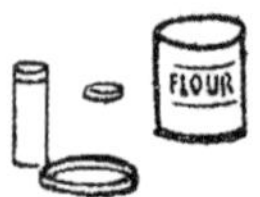

Common Pancakes

Make a light batter of eggs, flour and milk. Fry in a small pan, in hot dripping or lard. Salt, or nutmeg, and ginger, may be added. Sugar and lemon should be served to eat with them. Or when eggs are scarce make the batter with flour and a very little milk, will serve as well as egg.

Heat the frying pan tolerably hot. Wipe it with a clean cloth. Then pour in the batter, to make thin pancakes.

Hasty Pudding

Boil four bay leafs in a quart of milk. Beat up the yolk of two eggs and stir in a little salt with two or three spoonfuls of milk and stir into the milk, with a piece of butter.

Boil up the milk once, stirring all the time. Then stir in as much flour with a wooden spoon as will make it of a good thickness, taking care that in so doing you make it smooth: then, pour it into a deep dish and stick pieces of butter here and there.

Lounge Pudding

One pint cream, peel of one lemon, a little mace, sweeten to taste. Boil about a quarter of an hour, then take out the mace and peel, pound them fine and put through a sieve into the cream.

Beat up the yolks of eight eggs, stir all together, put it in a shape of proper size. Have ready a stewpan with boiling water that will hold it. Set the shape into the water, cover it quite close so as the steam cannot get in, boil it twenty-five minutes. Set it by to get cool. When nearly cold turn it into the dish it is intended to serve it up in and before sending to table pour over it about half a pint of currant jelly just warmed.

The shape should be cold and firm, which contrasted with the warm jelly makes it delicious.

Excellent Gooseberry Pudding

Coddle one quart green gooseberries, rub them through a hair sieve. Take six spoonfuls of the pulp, four eggs, quarter pound clarified butter, half pound powdered sugar, a little lemon peel shred fine and a little biscuit. Mix all together and bake them as a tart, with crust round the dish.

Superb Stewed Pears

Cover the pears with spring water and put them over a slow fire. Let them remain cooking till a dent can be made in them. Take them out and dry them. Peel them very thick and part them in halves. Take out the cores and save the pips. Boil the pips and peels in 3 pints water. Let it stand. Then take as much of the water as you deem sufficient and to 1 lb pears put 1 lb sugar. Put the pips with 4 cloves and a little cinnamon into a muslin bag with two pennyworth of cochineal, the juice and peel of two fine lemons. Stew one hour with the pears, add some brandy and continue to simmer three hours more till quite clear and red. 1 pint brandy to 9 lbs pears.

Mother's Golden Pippins Stewed

Take a quart of spring water; half a pound refined sugar; pippins as many as the liquor will cover, having been previously peeled quite smooth and laid in cold water. When the sugar and water begin to boil, put in the pippins and let them boil quick so as to be covered with a white froth. As soon as they are clear, pour in the juice of a lemon and the peel cut in long shreds. Boil a minute or two after. Then take them out and lay them in a dish. Let the liquor boil longer and when the apples are quite cold, pour it over them. The pippins are better for lying a day or so in the liquor. Keep the peel in the syrup or it will lose its colour.

Norfolk Plum Pudding

4 spoonfuls flour

½ lb currants

¼ lb loaf sugar

4 eggs and some lemon peel

1 lb plums

¾ lb suet

½ a nutmeg

Brandy 2 spoonfuls (or rum is richer)

Mix all together and boil for four hours. First mix eggs and flour, then plums and currants, then sugar, spice, etc., then brandy. Flour a mould and put it in with a spoon.

Lemon Cream

Take 5 lemons, pare them as thin as possible and steep all night in 20 spoonfuls soft water with the juice of the lemons. Then strain through a jelly bag into a silver saucepan. Beat the whites of six eggs well and add with 10 ozs fine sugar. Set it over a slow charcoal fire. Stir it all and skim; when as hot as will just bear the fingers in, pour it in glasses.

Trifle

Pour two ounces macaroons, two ounces of Savoy biscuits and two ounces of ratafia cakes into the trifle dish. Grate some nutmeg over and strew some lemon peel and bitter almonds cut fine on the cakes. Then pour in sufficient white wine to soften the cakes, and let them stand. For the custard take the yolk of four eggs, heat them on the fire and stir them till thick, but do not let them boil. When quite cold add one ounce of sweet almonds blanched and well beaten. Pour half a glass of brandy over the cakes and let them stand till next day, but make the syllabub immediately.

Mrs. Yarrington's Syllabub

One pint cream, lemon juice, a part of the peel, half a pint of white wine and sugar to taste. Pour it into a large bowl and whisk it. Have ready, covered with muslin, a sieve upon a dish to lay the froth on as it rises. Let it drain till next day. Then take it off the sieve with a spoon and lay it all over the custard. *If it does not look smooth on top, make some froth with a little sugar and cream.*

PRESERVES OF FRUIT

Preserves of Medlars

Take any quantity of medlars when they are quite ripe Put them in a preserving pan with as much water as will cover them. Let them simmer gently till they become a pulp. Then strain the liquor through a jelly bag till quite clear.

To every pint of liquor take ¾ lb fine sugar. Melt it down in the preserving pan to a thin syrup. Then boil it all together for two hours, or till it is found to jelly stiffly and put it in preserving glasses or small pots well warmed to receive it. Cover with paper while quite hot. Note. Tie the paper covers over the glasses or pots as soon as they are filled.

To scald codlings

Wrap each in a vine-leaf, and pack them close in a nice saucepan, and when full, pour as much water as will cover them. Set it over a gentle fire, and let them simmer slowly till done enough to take the thin skin off when cold. Place them in a dish, with or without milk, cream or custard; if the latter there should be no ratafia. Dust fine sugar over.

Bullace (Green Damson) Jelly

Put four pints bullaces into a quick oven or copper. Let them continue there till they give out one pint of juice. Strain it off and to the juice put one pound of fine sugar. Boil twenty minutes, skimming it all the time. Then having slightly oiled the moulds, pour the jelly in. *Mrs. Ives.*

Cherries, how to dry them

Cherries, twelve pounds; sugar, six pounds. Choose the fruit quite ripe without being too much so. Stone and stalk them. Put the pulps into a varnished pot by layers, at first a layer of cherries, then a layer of sugar till the pot be full. Leave the whole thus 48 hours for slight fermentation, after which put them into the pan and give them four boilings. Then put them to cool in a pot of varnished earth and leave them till next day, when they must be laid on withies to dry by the heat of the sun, or if it can't be had, in a stove or cool oven.

Great Grandmother's Recipe for Quince Cakes 1694

Coddle some quinces till tender, pare and slice them, rub the pulp through a hair sieve. To one pound of fruit, put one pound sugar. Beat both up together with a spoon in a basin until it be quite white and thick. Having some paper shapes ready, place the mixture therein and dry in a stove.

Currant Syrup

Red currants 3 lbs, cherries 1½ lbs, raspberries 1½ lbs, picked and passed through a tamy. Set by in cellar 24 hours. Then pass through a jelly bag. To 1 pint juice 1 lb sugar. Boil enough not to become syrup. Put in pint bottles. Don't cork, but cover them with paper pricked with pinholes.

Apricot Paste Dried

Choose some fine apricots. Peel them. Remove the stones. As done, put them in fresh water, and afterwards on the fire. Stir them up till in a marmalade. Then place them on a tamy to drain and when cold beat them up into a pulp, which must be reduced half by evaporation.

Place this in a china basin previously weighed, and against the pulp weigh an equal quantity of fine sugar. Boil to the little caffay in the apricot water and into it turn the pulp, stirring it well all the time. Then place it again on the fire, which must be gentle. Boil it and stir it till the bottom of the pan is seen. Then fill the moulds therewith. Smooth them with a knife. Powder them with sugar and put them in the oven.

Take them out next day, turn, powder and dry them again and then the next day put them in tin boxes to keep.

Mrs Day's Preserved Bottle Fruit

Gather fruit in on a dry day. Bottle same day. Shake it well into the bottles that they may be quite full. Cork so as to be perfectly air tight. Wire down the corks. Dip them in plaster paris, place them in a kettle of cold water, hay round their sides and deep enough to cover the shoulders of the bottles. Place the kettle on the fire. Cover with a wet cloth to prevent steam escaping. As soon as the water boils, take the kettle off the fire and let the bottle remain till cold. Then dip the corks in luting and set in a cool place.

Select bottles with perfectly round mouths, as contributive to security in corking.

SAVOURY DISHES

Macaroni

Boil till tender in milk and water. Then put it in a stewpan with some cream and a little butter, which thicken, if wanted, with a little flour. If cheese is added, grate a little into the stewpan with it, adding a little salt. Stew it for ten minutes over a gentle fire. Pour the macaroni upon a dish and over grate some more cheese and salamander it of a light brown.

Plovers Eggs

Put some hay in the pan. Set the eggs on end. Pour cold water on them and when it begins boiling continue them on for 20 minutes. Then spread a napkin on a dish and lay the eggs on till next day, when they may be either eaten or packed up.

Ramakins

Scrape a quarter of a pound of Cheshire and ditto of Gloucester cheese, ditto of good fresh butter; then beat all in a mortar with the yolks of four eggs and the inside of a small roll boiled in cream till soft; mix the paste then with the whites of the eggs previously beaten, and put into small paper pans made rather long than square, and bake in an oven till of a fine brown. They should be eaten quite hot. Some like the addition of a glass of white wine. *The batter for ramakins is equally good over macaroni when boiled tender; or on stewed celery, or cauliflower, a little of the gravy they have been stewed in being put in the dish with them, but not enough to make the vegetables swim.*

Cudgery, Breakfast Dish

A teacupful of rice boiled as for curry; same quantity of cold turbot or other fish; the hard boiled whites of 2 eggs; the yolks of 3. Cut the fish and eggs into dice and mix altogether with a little salt and cayenne. Heat it in a stewpan and serve.

Roast Cheese, to come up after dinner

Grate three ounces of fat Cheshire cheese. Mix it with the yolks of two eggs, four ounces of grated bread and three ounces of butter. Beat the whole well in a mortar, with a dessert-spoonful of mustard, and a little salt and pepper.

Toast some bread, cut it into proper pieces, lay the paste as above thick upon them, put them into a oven covered with a dish, till hot through. Remove the dish, and let the cheese brown a little. Serve as hot as possible.

Mushroom Loaves

Wash buttum mushrooms as for picking. Boil them a few minutes in water, and put to them two spoonfuls of cream, butter rolled in flour, salt and pepper. Boil these up. Then fill your loaves, and do them as directed for oyster loaves.

Oyster Loaves

Make a hole at the top of little round loaves to take out the crumb. Put some oysters into a stewpan with the liquor and the crumbs that were taken out of the loaves and a piece of butter. Stew them together, five or six minutes, then put in a spoonful of good cream and fill your loaves.

Lay a bit of crust on the top of each and put them in the oven to crisp.

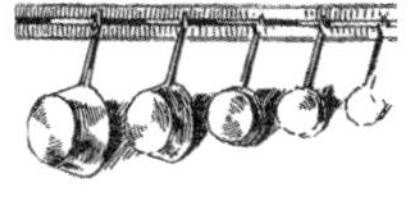

PRESERVES OF MEAT, etc.

To pot butter

To every pound of butter add ½ oz salt, ¼ oz salt petre and ¼ oz loaf sugar. Pot them down in 12 lb pots and cover close from air. Good in the spring.

Anchovy Butter

Butter two ozs; fix anchovies boned and pounded well in a mortar. Boil enough parsley to make it of a nice green colour. Mix it all together and make them into pats to serve with cheese. George IV.

To Send Cream Bottled

Fill the bottle with cream. Cork it lightly, put it on a saucepan in water and a bain marie and heat it. This will keep good some time.

Lord Hardwick had his cream always thus supplied.

To Pot Pigeons

Let them be quite fresh. Clean them carefully, and season them with salt and pepper. Lay them close in a small deep pan; for the smaller the surface and the closer they are packed, the less butter will be wanted. Cover them with butter, then with very thick paper tied down and bake them.

When cold, put them dry into pots that will hold two or three in each and pour butter over them, using that which was baked as part. Observe that the butter should be pretty thick over them, if they are to be kept.

If pigeons were boned and then put in an oval form into the pot, they would lie closer and require less butter.

They may be stuffed with a fine forcemeat made with bacon, etc. and then they will eat excellently. *If a high flavour is approved of, add mace, allspice, and a little Cayenne before baking.*

To Pot Salmon

Take a large piece, scale and wipe, but don't wash. Salt very well. Let it lie till the salt is melted and drained from it, then season with beaten mace, cloves and whole pepper. Lay in a few bay-leaves, put it close into a pan, cover it over with butter and bake it. When well done, drain it from the gravy, put it into the pots to keep, and when cold cover it with clarified butter.

In this manner you may do any firm fish.

To Pot Herrings

After having cleaned them, cut off the heads and lay them close in an earthen pot. Between every layer of herrings strew salt, but not too much: put in cloves, mace, whole pepper and pieces of nutmeg. Fill up the pan with vinegar, water and a quarter of a pint of white wine. Cover and tie it down, bake it, and when cold, pot it for use.

Force Meat, and Game Pie

Make a crust with 2 lbs well dried and sifted flour. Rub into this 8 ozs butter, till it becomes like crumbs of bread. Then, having beaten 3 eggs and their whites, with a little water and a pinch of salt, add them and make the whole into a stiff paste.

Roll this out to the thickness of about ¼ of an inch and dress the shape in which the pie is to be baked withal. Then make forced meat with 2½ lbs sausage meat previously seasoned, to which add afterwards the spice seasoning below and a spoonful and a half of fine chopped leek. Beat this all in a marble mortar till it becomes like potted meat; then, having boned and well spiced the game and fowls, put over the bottom crust of this pie a layer of bacon; then a layer of forced meat; then a fowl or the fowl cut in pieces; but beat the thick of the legs with the force meat, or lard them through and through. They will else be hard.

Fill up all the intervals with forcemeat and pieces of pork lard. Put over a layer of game. Fill up the intervals as before, placing always pieces of bacon against the walls of the pie, to keep the interior moist and so on till the pie is filled.

Cover the whole top with forced meat and over that slices of bacon.

Place on the crust over the top. Make a chimney in the top. Surround this with a fillet of crust to serve as a handle afterwards, when the top is removed.

Yellow the top with beaten yolk of egg and a pastry brush and ornament the whole with paste made of flour and water only, which baking white, contrasts nicely with the crust made yellowed by the yolk of egg.

Garnish the pie round with white paper frilled by being snipped with scissors on the top. Set it in a deep ragout dish with a napkin, smartly concealing the bottom and with it serve up savoury jelly.

Spice Seasoning for above

Allspice ½ oz, nutmeg ¼ oz, mace ¼ oz, 24 cloves and 2 ozs of the usual pepper and salt seasoning. Bake it.

To Make Sprats Taste Like Anchovies

Salt them well and let the salt drain from them. In twenty four hours wipe them dry, but don't wash them.

Mix four ounces of common salt, an ounce of baysalt, an ounce of saltpetre, a quarter of an ounce of sal-prunel and half a teaspoonful of cochineal; all in the finest powder. Sprinkle it among three quarts of the fish, and pack them in two stone jars. Keep in a cool place, fastened down with a bladder. These are pleasant on bread and butter, but use the best for sauce.

Force For Pies

Equal quantities of veal and fat of bacon, or of beef and bacon. Chop them together and season them with pepper, salt and allspice: but no herbs – which will not keep – if the pie into which it is to be put is required for keeping: but otherwise add parsley, shallots and fine herbs, truffles etc.

Turkey Stuffing

Crumb bread 8 ozs, suet 4 ozs, shallot chopped fine 2 teaspoons, powdered herbs 1 teaspoon, parsley and seasoning 1 teaspoon each, 1 egg, ¼ nutmeg and a blade of mace.

To Preserve Eggs

Water highly impregnated with lime will preserve them for two years. Some people put eggs in puddled lime and water, but the shells are often destroyed and the eggs rendered good for nothing.

Eggs may be also submitted twenty seconds to boiling water and then buried in sand.

PICKLES

To Make Vinegar With The Plant

Mix ¼ lb treacle with 3 pints water, to which add ½ lb brown sugar. Make it smoothly fluid and put it in a found earthen vessel that will hold it well, having a rim round the top so you can easily tie down some brown paper over it.

Leave the vinegar plant to float on the top and having covered it up with the paper put the pan in a moderately warm place and leave it thus six weeks. Then carefully remove the vinegar plant, pour off the vinegar, strain it through a sieve, boil and when cool bottle it; and keep for use.

The young plant must be carefully removed from the old one with a spoon and immediately placed in the new mixed fluid.

This vinegar is of the same delicate flavour as French white wine vinegar.

My Aunt's Pickle

Use cucumbers or melons. If the latter, cut out two of the sections in one slice and with a teaspoon scoop out the inside and wipe it well with a clean cloth. Put in a good deal of salt, and rub it well in the inside, so as to make it penetrate the substance. After the same manner rub the sections which were cut out. Put it on the top of a sieve and let it drain.

In two days' time take some ginger, whole pepper, horse radish sliced, mustard seed, garlic, shallots and a little cayenne pepper and having scalded some vinegar pout it over and into the melons. Scald also the ingredients in a little vinegar to swell them, fill the melons or cucumbers as full as possible with them.

In 24 hours after, scald some more vinegar and pour it over the pickle. Use salt to taste.

Pickled Mushrooms

Cut the stalk off some small buttons. Rub the skin with flannel dipped in salt. Throw them into milk and water. When all done, drain them and put them in a stewpan with salt sprinkled over them. Cover them close, put the over a gentle stove for five minutes to draw off the water. Then put them in a coarse cloth to drain till cold. Fill some large mouthed bottles with the buttons and fill up with white vinegar and a little mace.

To Dry Mushrooms

Wipe them clean and of the large take out the brown and peel off the skin. Lay them on paper to dry in a cool oven and keep them in paper bags, in a dry place. When used, simmer them in the gravy and they will swell to near their former size, to simmer them in their own liquor till it dry up into them, shaking the pan, then drying on tin plates, is a good way, with spice or not, as above, before made into powder. Tie down with bladder; and keep in a dry place, or in paper.

To Pickle Gherkins

Take five hundred gherkins. Put them in a pot, cover with spring water, to every gallon of which two pounds of salt has been put. Leave them two hours. Then boil with each gallon of vinegar half an ounce cloves and of mace, one ounce each, of allspice and mustard seed, a stick of horse radish cut in slices, six bay leafs, a little dill, two or three ounces of ginger, a nutmeg cut in pieces and a handful of salt. Boil them all together and pour them over the gherkins. Let them stand twenty-four hours and put them on a gentle fire to simmer till green, but on no account let them boil: after which set them by till cold and cover well with bladder and leather. Take them out with a wooden spoon. *Kidney beans are pickled the same as gherkins.*

To Pickle Onions

Take the smallest onions; silver skin are the best. When dry and fit to lay up for winter, put them in a pot of spring water with a handful of salt and let them boil up once. Then strain them off and take off of them three coats. Put them in a cloth and let two people take hold of them and rub them backward and forward till dry. Then put them in bottles, with plenty of mace, cloves, ginger and nutmeg cut in pieces, with also a good parcel of garlics. Boil up some double distilled white wine vinegar with some salt and when cold, pour it upon the onions. Cork them close and tie a bladder and leather over the bottles.

To Pickle Walnuts Black

Take some walnuts fullgrown, but before the shell is hard. Lay them in salt and water two days. Then put them in fresh salt and water two days more (2 lbs salt to 1 gallon water). Then in some more fresh water three days. Put them now into the pickle jars. When half full put in a large onion stuck with cloves. To one hundred walnuts put half a pint mustard seed, or salt a quarter of an ounce, of mace a quarter of ounce, half an ounce black pepper, and of long pepper, half an ounce allspice, six bay leaves and a stick of horse radish. Then fill the jar and pour upon them the boiling vinegar. Cover them with a plate and when cold tie them down with bladder and leather. In three months they will be fit to eat.

Ketchup, to Keep for Twenty Years

Take two gallon of stale strong beer or ale, the stronger and staler the better; a pound of anchovies washed and cleaned; half an ounce each of mace and cloves; a quarter of an ounce of pepper; six races of ginger; a pound of shallots and two quarts of flap mushrooms, rubbed and picked. Boil these over a slow fire one hour; then strain the liquor through a flannel bag and let it stand till cold; it must be bottled and stopped close with cork and bladder or leather.

One spoonful of this ketchup is sufficient to put to a pint of melted butter. It is, by many, preferred to the best Indian soy.

Mock Ginger

Take very large cauliflowers. First pick the flowers from the stalks, peel, throw them into strong brine for three days, drain and put them in a jar. Boil white wine vinegar with cloves, mace, long pepper and allspice, half an ounce of each, forty blades of garlic, a stick of horse-radish, sliced, a quarter of an ounce of Cayenne pepper a quarter of a pound of yellow turmeric and two ounces of bay salt.

Pour it over the stalks boiling hot, cover it close till next day, then boil it again and repeat it twice more, when cold, tie it down close.

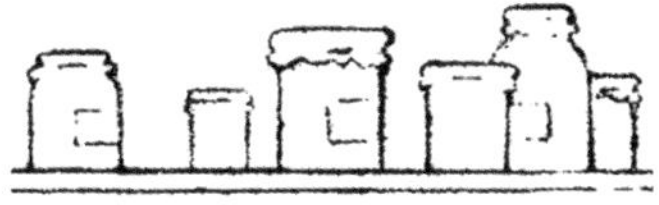

SAUCES

A Good White Sauce for Fowls

Boil 4 ozs of rice in 1 pint of new milk. Add onion sliced and seasoning. When done rub through a sieve. Then beat up a little cream with the yolk of an egg. Mix and warm all together and use.

Plum Sauce for Roast Pig

Boil some currants till soft. Then take some bread which has been soaking in boiling milk wherein was some mace; put into a saucepan with a glass of white wine and the currants, beat them together and serve up.

From My Great Grandmother's recipe book, 1694.

To Make Parsley Sauce When No Parsley Leaves are to be had

Tie up a little parsley-seed in a bit of muslin and boil it ten minutes in some water. Use this water to melt the butter; and throw into it a little boiled spinach minced, to look like parsley.

A Very Fine Mushroom Sauce

Wash and pick a pint of young mushrooms and rub them with salt, to take off the tender skin. Put them in a saucepan with a little salt, some nutmeg, a blade of mace, a pint of cream, and a good piece of butter rubbed in flour. Boil them up and stir them till done; then pour it round the chickens etc. Garnish them with lemon.

If you cannot get fresh mushrooms, use pickled ones down white, with a little mushroom-powder with the cream, etc.

The Old Currant Sauce for Venison

Boil an ounce of dried currants in half a pint of water a few minutes; then add a small teacupful of breadcrumbs, six cloves, a glass of port-wine and a bit of butter. Stir it till the whole is smooth.

Tomato Sauce

When the tomatoes are ripe put them whole into a gently warm oven. Let them remain there till soft as a roasted apple. Scrape the pulp from the skin with a silver spoon, carefully avoiding touching it with the fingers. Rub the pulp through a fine sieve, (but not the watery liquor). Put to this as much chilli or common vinegar as will make it of a proper consistence and to every quart of liquor put one ounce of garlic, two ounces of shallots, a small quantity of ginger; all sliced thin. Add salt and cayenne as preferred. Boil all together very gently till it is the thickness of cream. Strain it through a cullender and bottle for use. If it should ferment, boil it a short time again with a little salt.

Horse Radish Sauce

Teaspoonful mustard, tablespoonful vinegar, 3 tablespoons thick cream, a little salt, as much horse radish grated into it as will make it as thick (as onion sauce) and a little shallot and (if relished) garlic.

A Very Fine Fish Sauce

Put into a very nice tin saucepan a pint of fine port wine, a gill of mountain, half a pint of fine walnut-ketchup, twelve anchovies and the liquor that belongs to them, a gill of walnut-pickle, the rind and juice of a large lemon, four or five shallots, some Cayenne to taste, three ounces of scraped horse radish, three blades of mace, and two tea-spoonfuls of made mustard.

Boil it all gently, till the rawness goes off; then put it into small bottles for use. Cork them very close and seal the top.

Harvey's Sauce

Take 12 anchovies, 2 heads garlic, 3 heads shallots, small teaspoonful of cochineal powdered. Chop these well all together and very fine; to them put two quarts vinegar. Boil all together till the anchovies are quite dissolved. Add then 5 spoonfuls walnut pickle and a teaspoonful of Cayenne pepper. Boil them and let them stand 10 days in a covered jar and then pass the liquor through a lawn sieve and bottle for use. *Mrs. Knatchbull's recipe.*

A Gravy Without Meat

Put a glass of small beer, a glass of water, some pepper, salt, lemon-peel (grated), a bruised clove or two and a spoonful of walnut pickle, or mushroom ketchup, into a basin. Slice an onion, flour and fry it in a piece of butter till it is brown.

Then turn all the above into a small toffer with the onion, and simmer it covered twenty minutes. Strain it off for use and when cold take off the fat.

Gravy to Make Mutton Eat, Like Venison

Pick a very stale woodcock or snipe, cut it to pieces (but first take out the bag from the entrails) and simmer with as much unseasoned meat gravy as you will want. Strain it, and serve in the dish.

Useful and Entertaining Knowledge

To melt butter: this is rarely well done, though a very essential article.

Mix in the proportion of a tea-spoonful of flour to four ounces of the best butter on a trencher.

Put it into a small saucepan and two or three tablespoonfuls of hot water. Boil quick a minute, shaking it all the time. Milk used instead of water required rather less butter and looks white.

HOME BREWERY AND WINES

Excellent Cheap Beer

Boil 8 gallons water and when cooled to 176 degrees, or so hot as only to pain the finger sharply when put into it, stir into it one bushel of ground malt; mash it three hours and then draw off. Then pour upon the grains 8 gallons more water at 196 degrees or rather hotter. Let it mash two hours and draw off. Then mash the grains with 8 gallons more water. Let it stand one hour and a half and draw off. Then mix 28 lbs treacle in 20 gallons water and having damped 2 lbs hops, put the wort, treacle and water and hops all together for two hours, stirring it as long as the hops float. Then let it cool, and when about milk warm mix half a pint of yeast in about 2 gallons of beer. Stir it well. Leave it to work and then add it to the whole quantity, cover it with sacks and let it work 24 hours. Then put it in the barrel, keep filling up and in 3 days bung up. In 3 days draw it off into another barrel to clear it from what has been deposited like lees at the bottom of the barrel and which in bad cellars creates at all changes of re-fermentation. In no case use *boiling* water.

	s.d.
1 Bush Malt	9.0
28 lbs treacle	8.2
2 lbs hops	3.0
£1 : 0 : 2 for 1¾ per quart	

To Refine Ale or Beer

Whites and shells 12 eggs, 1 oz salt tartar, ½ oz pearl ash, ½ oz grains paradise bruised salt fine, and mix with these as much whiting as will make it of a thick paste. Roll this into small balls. Put these into the bung hole and flop stop down immediately.

In a few days thick and sour beer will thus become pleasant. The above is quantity sufficient for a hogshead. *Moore's Almanack, 1827.*

Mrs. Hall's Recipe for Hop Barm

Boil two ounces of hops in two gallons water until the hops sink. Take four pounds potatoes boiled and peeled and rub them through a sieve with two quarts water. Add two tablespoonfuls of brown sugar to the above. Put it in a jar and leave it before the fire during twenty-four hours, at the end of which time it will be fit for use. *Tours, 1826*

Queen Elizabeth's Metheglin

Sweet briar leafs, one bushel, thyme, one bushel, rosemary half a bushel, bay leaves one peck. Put these in about twenty gallons of water, and boil them fifteen minutes, after which, pour it through a fine cloth and to every gallon of honey, put one gallon of this liquor.

Then beat the whole together an hour's space, after which boil it as long as any scum rises. Then pour it off again through a cloth into a kive or tub and when of the proper warmth, put it into the barrel and work it with some yeast spread on toast and after, tun it up when done working and keep it twelve month before bottling.

Note. We found this fulsomely rich, so put 2 gallons water to one of honey. Bottle Metheglin or Mead always in pint bottles, as it gets flat when once uncorked. Extract from an old booke of Sr. Jnr. Moore's.

Miss Blomefield's Small Mead

Water six gallons, honey nine pounds. Beat the whites of four eggs and mix the ingredients when cold. Then put them on the fire and skim while boiling. Having boiled half an hour put it into a pot or kive, and when milk-warm work it with barm on a toast. When full working take out the toast and add the juice of a lemon and lemon peel to each gallon.

Next day rack it into clean bottles lightly corked. After three days put it into fresh ones clear from the sediment and cork for use in fourteen days.

Potato Brandy Equal to Cognac

Potatoes well washed, fifty pounds. Dress them by steam. Bruise them with a roller to powder. Take two pounds malt, ground coarse, steep it in luke warm water, pour it into the fermenting bath and pour on it six quarts boiling water. Stir it and throw in the potato powder. Stir it again till every part of the potatoes is well saturated. Immediately four or five ounces of barm is to be mixed with fourteen gallons of hot water sufficiently warm to make the whole when mixed from 59 to 66 degrees. Then add half a pint of good brandy. The fermenting bath must be placed in a room kept by means of a stove or otherwise to the warmth at a temperature of 66 degrees to 72 degrees. The mixture must be covered and left to rest and will rise in the vessel 6 or 8 inches for which allowance must be made on putting it in the bath. Leave it thus five or six days, when if the liquor is clear and the potatoes fallen to the bottom, decant the fluid and distil by vapour. This ought to yield 3 quarts and when burnt sugar is added to it, cannot be distinguished from French Brandy. *The residue is good for cattle.*

1827 British Wine

Unripe grapes, forty pounds, picked from the stalks. Bruise them in a mortar but do not break the seeds. Put them in a tub just covering them with water. At the end of the second put them to press. Dissolve 36 or 40 pounds sugar in water sufficient to make the quantity ten gallons.

In two or three days draw off the liquor free from sediment by a peg in the side of the tub near the bottom and put it in the cask in the cellar. Put on the bung slightly at first but when safe drive it in hard, giving vent at the peghole. Let it remain in the cask till March twelve month and then rack it off into a well sulphured cask containing lees of wine, or such substances as are intended to flavour it. Let it remain another year. If necessary fine it and bottle if off. *Keep it in bottle two years and it will be mistaken for foreign wine.*

Cowslip Wine

To every gallon of water, weigh three pounds of lump sugar. Boil the quantity half an hour, taking off the scum as it rises. When cool enough, put to it a crust of toasted bread dipped in thick yeast. Let the liquor ferment in the tub thirty-six hours, then into the cask put, for every gallon, the peel of two and rind of one lemon, and both of one Seville orange and one gallon of cowslip-pips, then pour on them the liquor. It must be carefully stirred every day for a week: then to every five gallons put in a bottle of brandy. Let the cask be close stopped and stand only six weeks before you bottle off. *Observe to use the best corks.*

Gooseberry Champagne

To every pound of gooseberries, full-gown but not coloured, well crushed, add one pint cold soft water. Let them stand till they begin to ferment. Then press out the liquor and to every quart of it add one pound loaf sugar. Fill the cask quite full and keep it full up to the bung hole so that the scum and yeast may work out.

When the strong fermentation is over, but before it has done hissing, add to every nine gallons, half an oz isinglass dissolved in cold cider and let it be well stirred about for 15 minutes, after which the wine must not be disturbed, but as soon as it is fine it must bottled in strong champagne bottles and wired down. October, 1832.

Lemon Juice, To Preserve

Put to three bottles of lemon juice one of rum. To be made when fruit is cheap. Keep it in cellar.

Rum Booze - Christ's College, Cambridge

Yolks of 4 eggs well beaten with powdered sugar therein in a basin.

Take ½ bottle of sherry. Add thereto grated peel of ½ a lemon, ½ nutmeg grated, a piece of cinnamon and some sugar. Put the whole in a saucepan on the fire. When it boils take it off. Put in a vessel with a spout to it and add 1 glass of rum. Pour this gradually on the eggs, sweeten to taste and beat to a white froth before serving. *Excellent for Christmas*

Cyder Cup – Trinity Hall, Cambridge

Four tablespoons of sifted sugar

Two bottles cyder

One bottle Madeira

A teacupful (i.e. about ¼ pint) each of brandy, noyau, rum shrub and sherry.

Mix all well together. Then take a lump of bread that has been hard dried in toasting (without burning) three hours before. Put this in and a lemon sliced thin, and over all grate half a nutmeg. Exquisite. Given me by the Butler. June 1842.

In college the person who drinks stands up and so also the man on his left, whom he drinks to as pledge, and thus everyone in succession stand up, two at a time.

CAPTAIN FRAYER'S PUNCH
One of sour,

Two of sweet,

Four of strong

Eight of weak.

An Excellent Method of Making Punch

Take two large fresh lemons with rough skins, quite ripe and some large lumps of double-refined sugar. Rub the sugar over the lemons till it has absorbed all the yellow part of the skins. Then put into the bowl these lumps and as much more as the juice of the lemons may be supposed to require; for no certain weight can be mentioned, as the acidity of a lemon cannot be known till tried and therefore this must be determined by the taste. Then squeeze the lemon-juice upon the sugar; and with a bruiser press the sugar and juice well together. The richness and fine flavour of the punch depends on this rubbing and mixing process being thoroughly performed.

Then mix this up very well with boiling water (soft water is best) till the whole is rather cool.

When this mixture (*which is now called the sherbet*) is to your taste, take brandy and rum in equal quantities and put them to it, mixing well together again. As the pulp is disagreeable to some persons, the sherbet may be strained before the liquor is put in.

When only rum is used, about half a pint of porter will soften the punch; and even when both rum and brandy are used, the porter gives a richness and to some a very pleasant flavour.

This receipt is greatly admired amongst the writer's friends. It is impossible to take too much pains in all the processes of mixing.

Milk Punch

1 quart new milk, 6 eggs beaten, 3 ozs sugar, 2 large wine glassfuls old rum (more can be added if wished strong) 1 nutmeg grated and the peel of a lemon, parred.

Process: Boil the milk, sugar, nutmeg and lemon peel together five or ten minutes. Then pour it to the beaten eggs, stirring well all the time. Add the rum, and having heated the punch bowl near the fire, pour the mixture into it from a height to make it froth and serve up.

Shrub

Of brandy and rum one pint, of orange juice one pint and a half, of lemon juice half a pint, of fine sugar a pound and one quarter. Steep the peel of one of the oranges and of one of the lemons in the spirit for two days. Then add the juice and the sugar. Shake it up now and then and after eight days strain it through a flannel bag and filter it for use.

Orgeat

Boil a quart of new milk with a stick of cinnamon, sweeten to your taste and let it grow cold; then pour it by degrees to three ounces of almonds, and twenty bitter, that have been blanched and beaten to a paste, with a little water to prevent oiling. Boil all together, and stir till cold, then add half a glass of brandy.

Nectar

Loaf sugar one pound, raisins chopped fine two pounds, two lemons, peel and juice.

Pour upon these ingredients two gallons boiling water, let it stand three or four days, stirring it well twice each day. Then strain and bottle it in stone bottles. It will be fit to drink in a fortnight and will keep 10 months. *Sir Thomas Gooch.*

Caudle for the Sick and Lying-in

Set three quarts of water on the fire; mix smooth as much oatmeal as will thicken the whole with a pint of cold water; when boiling, pour the latter in and twenty peppers in fine powder; boil to a good middling thickness; then add sugar, half a pint of well fermented table-beer, and a glass of gin. Boil all. This mess twice and once or twice of broth, will be of incalculable service.

Useful and Entertaining Knowledge

There is not a better occasion for charitable consideration than when a person is sick. A bit of meat or pudding sent unexpectedly has often been the means of recalling long-lost appetite. Nor are the indigent alone the grateful receivers; for in the highest houses a real good sick-cook is rarely met with; and many who possess all the goods of fortune, have attributed the first return of health to an appetite excited by good 'kitchen-physic', as it is called.

COURSES FOR A LITTLE DINNER PARTY OF TEN

FIRST COURSE

Clear Vermecelli Soup

remove,

Beef larded (Poiffade Sauce).

Veal Cutlets	Blanquette of Fowl
(*à la Dreux*).	(with cucumbers).
Rice Cafferoles	Mutton Patties
(*à la Reine*).	(*à l'Italienne*).
Ducklings	Fillets of Leveret (larded)
(*à la Macedonie*).	with Tomatoe Sauce.

Boiled and Fried Soles
Ribs of Lamb.

SECOND COURSE

Guinea Fowls (one larded).

remove,

French Fritters.

Potatoes	Celery with Marrow &
(*à la Maitre d'hotel*).	Spanifh Sauce.
Cherry Tartlets	Meringues
(*à la Crême*).	(*à la Chantilly*).
Sea Kale.	Lobster Salad.

Roast Pigeons.

remove,

Cake à la Ducheffe.

RATE OF WAGES FOR FEMALE DOMESTICS

	Higheſt Wages			Loweſt Wages		
	£	s.	d.	£	s.	d.
Houſekeeper	36	15	0	21	0	0
Lady's Maid	21	0	0	12	12	0
Upper Nurſe	20	0	0	10	10	0
Under Nurſe	12	12	0	6	6	0
Nursery Girl	6	6	0	4	4	0
Cook	20	0	0	10	10	0
Kitchen maid	12	12	0	8	8	0
Scullion	8	8	0	4	4	0
Upper houſemaid	12	12	0	8	8	0
Under houſemaid	9	9	0	6	6	0
Still maid	9	9	0	7	7	0
Laundry maid	14	14	0	10	10	0
Wet nurſe	26	5	0	18	18	0
Maid of all work	12	12	0	7	7	0

Note.   Tea and ſugar are allowed.

Mrs. Parkes, 1841

FISH TABLE (London)

In and Out of Season	January	February	March	April	May	June
Cod	IN	IN	IN	IN	IN	IN
Crabs	IN	IN	IN	IN	IN	IN
Flounders ..	OUT	IN	IN	IN	IN	IN
Herring	OUT	OUT	OUT	IN	IN	IN
Haddock	IN	IN	OUT	OUT	OUT	OUT
Lobster	IN	IN	IN	IN	IN	IN
Mackerel ..	—	—	—	—	IN	IN
Oysters	IN	IN	IN	IN	—	—
London Salmon	IN	IN	IN	IN	IN	IN
Soles	—	—	—	IN	IN	IN
Shrimps	IN	IN	IN	IN	IN	—
Sturgeon.. ..	—	—	IN	IN	IN	IN
Skate	IN	IN	IN	IN	IN	IN
Sprats	IN	IN	—	—	—	—
Turbot	—	—	IN	IN	IN	IN
Whiting	IN	IN	IN	—	—	—
Conger Eel ..	—	—	IN	IN	IN	IN
Plaice	IN	IN	IN	IN	IN	IN
Pike	IN	IN	—	—	—	—

FISH TABLE (London)

In and Out of Season	July	August	September	October	November	December
Cod	OUT	OUT	OUT	IN	IN	IN
Crabs	IN	OUT	OUT	IN	IN	IN
Flounders	IN	IN	IN	OUT	OUT	OUT
Herring	IN	IN	IN	IN	OUT	OUT
Haddock	OUT	OUT	OUT	IN	IN	IN
Lobster	OUT	OUT	IN	IN	IN	IN
Mackerel	IN	IN	—	—	—	—
Oysters	—	IN	IN	IN	IN	IN
London Salmon	IN	IN	—	—	IN	IN
Soles	IN	IN	IN	—	—	—
Shrimps	—	—	IN	IN	—	IN
Sturgeon	IN	IN	—	—	—	—
Skate	IN	—	—	—	IN	IN
Sprats	—	—	—	—	—	IN
Turbot	IN	IN	—	—	—	—
Whiting	—	—	—	IN	IN	IN
Conger Eel	IN	IN	IN	IN	—	—
Plaice	IN	IN	IN	—	—	IN
Pike	—	—	—	IN	IN	IN

MISCELLANEOUS USEFUL RECIPES

Sorrel, its uses and virtues

Sorrel goeth further into the earth than any other plant and therefore draws its nourishment without detriment to other plants, and suffers rarely, therefore, from frost. It is one of the wholesomnest herbs that can be eaten being antiscrobutic, creates appetites, represses bile and allays thirst.

Consumptive habits

A handful of leaves boiled in a pint of whey is an excellent medicine in April. The juice hereof relieves persons who spit blood and is excellent for all consumptive habits.

Sorrel is excellent with port and substitutes well for apples when eaten with goose.

Good Henry or Fat Hen

Good to lay on green wounds, when bruised to cleanse them. The leafs of this plant rubbed on warts takes them away.

Hyssop. Its Virtues

When boiled, excellent as a cataplasm for bruises, recovering the tone and colour of the flesh in a few hours. Taken in tea is good for coughs and disorders of the lungs. Hedge hyssop is too potent, unless boiled in milk, when it is good for the eyes. The tops should be tied in a cloth and afterwards boiled and applied warm at going to bed, the eye being shut. It is more effective when boiled in brine. The vapour of it is good in ringing of the ears.

To Keep Flowers in Water

Put a little camphor in the water, or saltpetre.

House-Leek. Its Virtues.

Good for heat and sharpness of wine when drank. Good for burns and scalds, also St. Anthony's fire, chapped hands and the safest cosmetic for the face, removing sun burns, freckles, etc.

Tansy

Tansy formerly was thought necessary to correct the nature of a Lent diet, and was much eaten at that time; but since keeping Lent is now too universally laid aside this, as well as other ancient customs, is laid by. It relieves the stomach of phlegm occasioned by a fish and pulse diet.

Preventive of Fever, etc.

Powdered nitre, six drachms, oil vitrio, six drachms. Mix in a tea cup, by adding one drachm of the oil at a time. The cup to be placed on a hot hearth or piece of heated iron during mixture and stir it up with a tobacco pipe or piece of glass. The cup to be changed to different parts of the room of the sick.

Valuable Fumigation Powder

Nitre, four lbs, sulphur, two lbs, southern wood and juniper berries, each three lbs; tar and myrrh, each, one 1lb and a half.

This was used by Mr. McGregor at Jersey where fifty men of the 80th Regiment were quickly lost by putrid fever before fumigation. But immediately after, not only malignant symptoms abated, but men then sick in hospital all recovered, who doubtless would have fallen a sacrifice to the disorder.

Cold Cream

Spermaceti, six drachms; white wax, six drachms;
oil almonds, six drachms; rose water, two pints.
Put these into a basin placed in a pan in
which there is boiling water. When all is
melted beat it up with a silver spoon till cold,
and add fresh rose water.

A Remedy for Blistered Feet

Mix the grease dropped from a lighted candle
in the hand with a little spirits and on going
to bed run the blisters therewith and they
will disappear before morning.
This remedy was used commonly by soldiers
in Napoleon's Imperial Guard. 1824

To Prevent Green Hay from Firing

Stuff a sack as full of straw or hay as possible. Tie
the mouth with a cord; and make the rick round
the sack, drawing it up as the rick advances in
height and quite out when finished.
The funnel thus left in the centre preserves it.

Dr. Impy's Remedy for Sea Sickness

Take a calomel pill day before, so as to have the
bowels clear. Then put one drop of creosote to
half a wine glass of brandy and water and drink
when getting qualmy.

To Choose Eggs at Market

Put the large end of the egg to your tongue; if it feels warm it is new. In new-laid eggs, there is a small division of the skin from the shell, which is filled with air, and is perceptible to the eye at the end. On looking through them against the sun or a candle, if fresh, eggs will be pretty clear. If they shake they are not fresh.

Ointment for the back of a Ricketty child

Pick a quantity of snails out of their shells and prick them full of holes; hang them up in a cloth and place a basin beneath to catch the liquor which drops from them; in this, when enough is obtained, must be boiled an ounce of spermaceti and half an ounce of powdered mace. With the ointment thus prepared rub all along the back-bone of the child, and round the neck, wrists and ankles, night and morning, chasing it well in by the fire every time. 1835

Shoe Blacking

Two table spoonfuls sweet oil, four ounces ivory black; three ounces spirit lavender; four ounces treacle, which, before it is added, must be mixed up with the fourth part of one quart vinegar, and two ounces of white sugar, three (or two) ounces oil of vitriol; when add the remainder of the vinegar.

Note. Spirits of Lavender not necessary but for smell. 3 ozs oil vitrio burns the leather without the lavender. George, from 3rd Kings Own Drgns.

Serjeant Garnam's Black Ink

Blue galls of Aleppo 4 oz., to be beaten in a mortar but not too small, to which put one quart of rain or river water, which place in an earthen vessel and stir every day for a month's space, keeping it in a warm situation, when, take of green copperas 1 oz to strike the colour with and after one day, of gum arabic 1 oz, to which may be added a little clear allum and it will be fit for use.

Sharpening Razors

The best mode of sharpening razors, etc. is by taking the rough side of a sharp skin such as bookbinders use, and rubbing this with pewter till the leather becomes glossy. Pass the edge over this half a dozen time circularly and it will do.

Wood Polish

Camphorated spirits, wine, one pint; gum shellac, half an ounce; gum copal, half an ounce; gum lac, half an ounce; gum landrich, a quarter of an ounce. Place in a gentle heat, shaking frequently till the gums are dissolved. It is then fit for use. Mall a roll of lint, put a little of the polish upon it and cover that with a soft linen rag slightly touched with linseed oil. Rub them into the wood in a circular form, not covering too large a space of wood at a time, till the pores become saturated, after which, rub in, in the same manner, spirits, wine with a small portion of polish added to it and a most brilliant polish will ensure.

Count Rumford's Mode of Lighting a Fire

A layer of fresh coals at bottom, a layer of kindling next and then on top the cinders, large first and little after.

Best Mode of Washing Silk Hose

Take sufficient quantity of soft rain water and after boiling it, mix with it some good white soap so as to make a strong wash. Pour some of this into a hand basin or other vessel of sufficient size and when only luke-warm put in the feet of the hose and let them soak some time; when squeeze, but do not rub, the dirty parts, and having thus got out the first dirt, put out the dirty water and take fresh, letting it stand as before till luke-warm.

Squeeze again the whole stockings and thus proceed till quite clean.

In the last wash, tied up in a little flannel bag, put in the colouring called cutbear, then spread the hose between towels quite even and let them dry entirely free from air.

Other Copper Beech Gift Books to collect:

THE LADY'S DRESSING ROOM

Open the door to beauty and relaxation secrets from days gone by. How to get up, fresh, beautiful and in an amiable frame of mind - with all your wrinkles smoothed over - and other fragrant tips from a golden age!

HOW TO ENTERTAIN YOUR GUESTS

A 1911 collection of indoor games.
A companion book to 'The Duties of Servants'.

THE DUTIES OF SERVANTS

The routine of domestic service in 1890.
Reproduced for your enjoyment now.

TEA; AN EVERYDAY INDULGENCE

Showing - how to enjoy tea: friends for tea, how to create tea time treats, uses of tea leaves, tea time trivia, amusements and good taste.

THE LADY'S BOOK OF MANNERS

Instructions showing how to be a perfect lady.

How to talk correctly, common errors corrected,

polite conversation, love, courtship and marriage.

SOCIAL SUCCESS

The modern girl's guide to confidence, poise,

manners and tact.

1930s etiquette for all occasions.

ETIQUETTE FOR GENTLEMEN

THE ETIQUETTE OF MOTORING

RECIPES FOR GARDENERS

DON'TS FOR GARDENERS

RECIPES FOR ROSES

ENGLISH LAVENDER

For your free catalogue containing
these and other titles write to:
Copper Beech Publishing
PO Box 159 East Grinstead Sussex RH19 4FS UK
www.copperbeechpublishing.co.uk

Copper Beech Gift Books
are designed and printed
in Great Britain.